AF428228

WHAT'S IN JERUSALEM? THE STORY OF THE CRUSADES

HISTORY BOOK FOR 11 YEAR OLDS
CHILDREN'S HISTORY

In this book, we're going to talk about the story of the
Crusades and their connection with the city of Jerusalem.
So, let's get right to it!

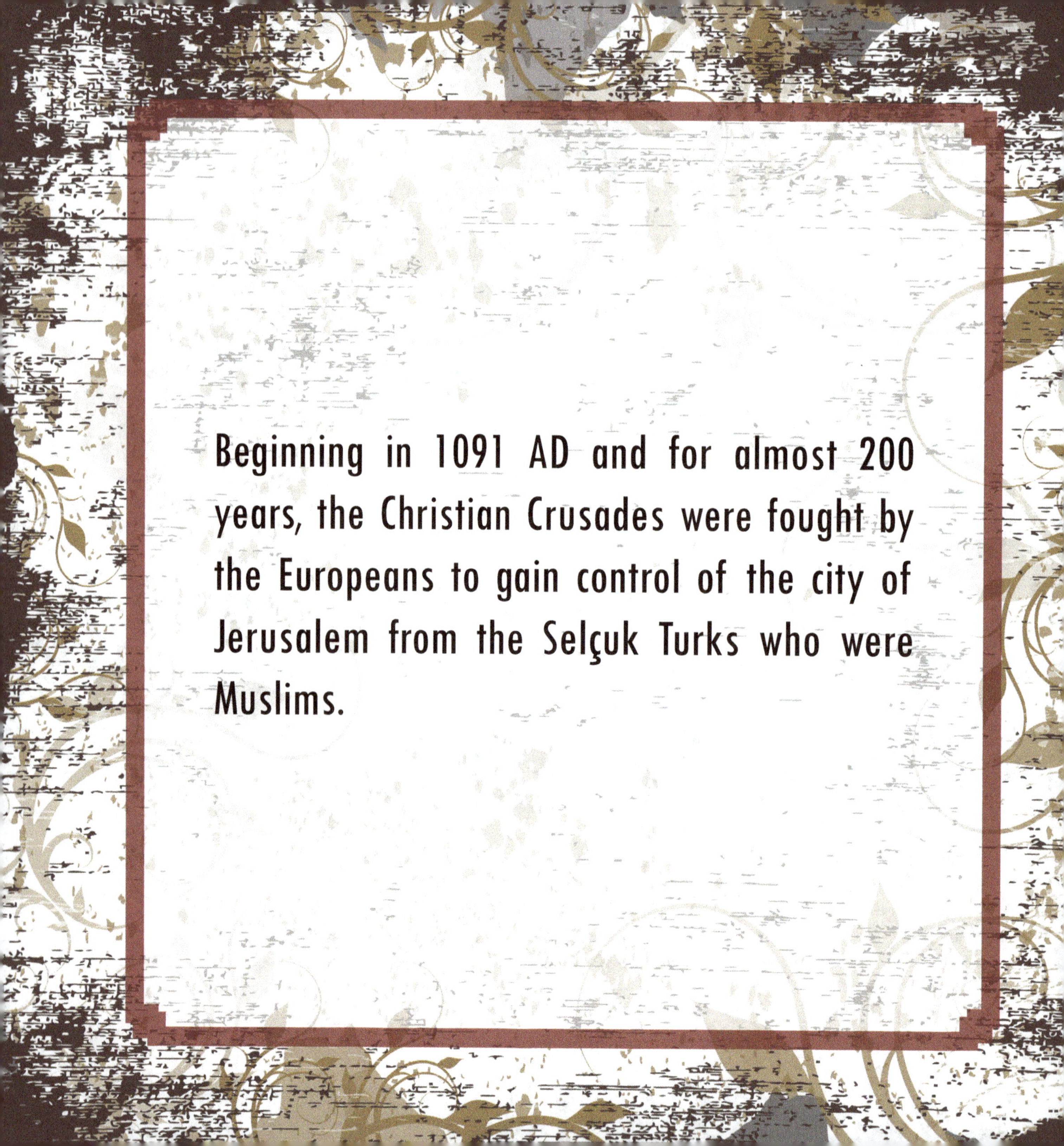

Beginning in 1091 AD and for almost 200 years, the Christian Crusades were fought by the Europeans to gain control of the city of Jerusalem from the Selçuk Turks who were Muslims.

Old city of Jerusalem

Christ at the Cross

WHY WAS JERUSALEM IMPORTANT?

Jerusalem was and is important to three religions—Christianity, Judaism, and Islam. It's important to Christians because they believe it was where Christ died on the cross and arose into heaven.

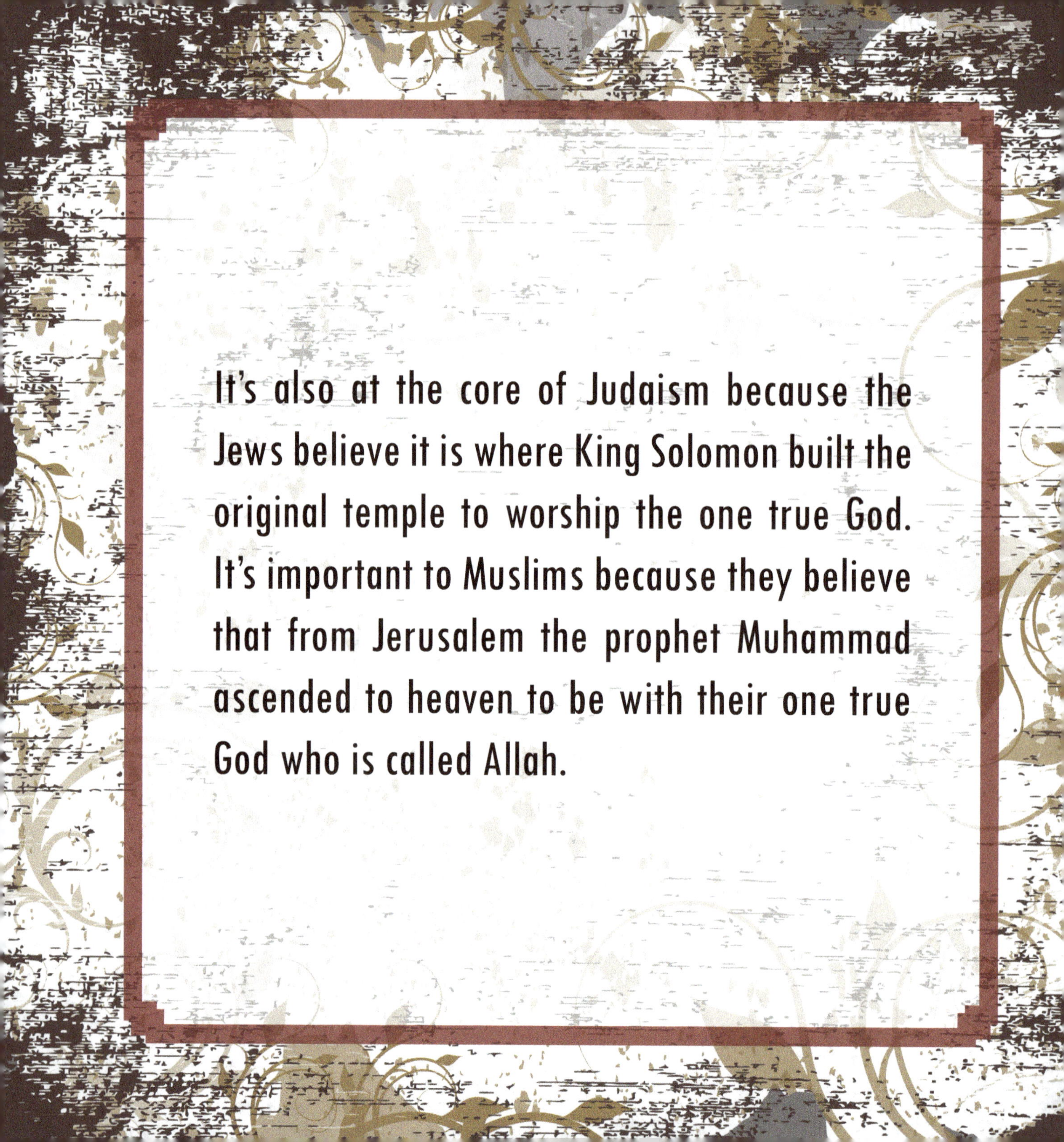

It's also at the core of Judaism because the Jews believe it is where King Solomon built the original temple to worship the one true God. It's important to Muslims because they believe that from Jerusalem the prophet Muhammad ascended to heaven to be with their one true God who is called Allah.

King Solomon Temple

WHAT WERE THE CRUSADES?

Movies have glorified the soldiers of the Crusades as powerful and gallant knights doing the work of God to save and protect the Holy Land. The truth is a lot less beautiful. The Crusades were a series of invasions and battles in the Holy Land that were fought by all different types of Europeans, most of whom weren't professional soldiers or knights. During the 200 years that the Crusades were fought, the Christians only had control of Jerusalem for approximately 90 years.

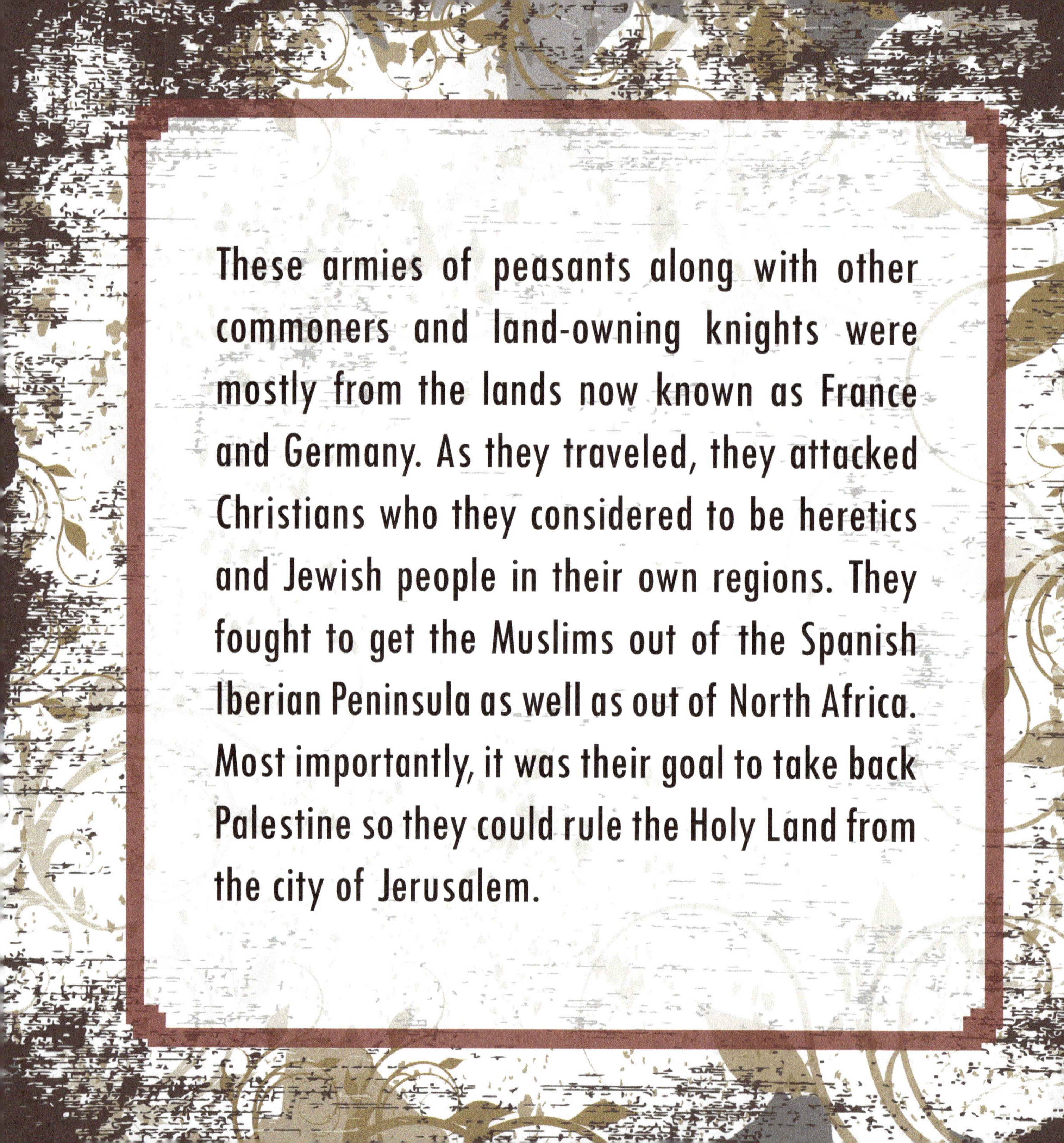

These armies of peasants along with other commoners and land-owning knights were mostly from the lands now known as France and Germany. As they traveled, they attacked Christians who they considered to be heretics and Jewish people in their own regions. They fought to get the Muslims out of the Spanish Iberian Peninsula as well as out of North Africa. Most importantly, it was their goal to take back Palestine so they could rule the Holy Land from the city of Jerusalem.

Holy Land

Amisos
Trapezus
Gangra
Amaseia
PONTUS
Euchaita
Dazimon
Koloneia
Satala
Sebasteia
Kamacha
Hisn Kamakh
Keltzine
Charsianon
Derzene
Basilika Therma
Tephrike
Chozanon
Nyssa
Tzamandos
LESSER ARMENIA
CAPPADOCIA
Halys
Caesarea
Taranton
al-Turanda
PASS OF
MELITENE
Charpete
Hisn Ziyad
Arsamosata
Simsat
Kyzistra
Sarus
THUGHUR
Melitene
Malatya
Nazianzos
Komana
Arabissos
Afsin
Koron
al-Qurra
Kiskisos
Sozopetra
Hisn Zibatra
Hisn Qalawdiya
Tyana
Rhodenton
Koukousos
AL-JAZIRIYA
Hisn Mansur
Amida
Diyar Bakr
Thebasa
Loulon
Lu'lu'a
Podandos
al-Nadandun
PASS OF
HADATH
Heraclea Cybistra
Sisium
Sisiya
Adata
al-Hadath
AL-JAZIRA
(UPPER
MESOPOTAMIA)
Hisn al-Saqaliba
CILICIAN
GATES
Samosata
Sumaysat
CILICIA
THUGHUR
Germanikeia
Mar'ash
Kaisun
Anabarzus
Ayn Zarba
al-Haruniya
Doliche
Duluk
Edessa
Adana
AL-SHAMIYA
Mopsuestia
al-Massisa
Cyrrhus
Qurus
Harran
Tarsus
Pyramus
AL-AWASIM
Seleucia
Alexandretta
Hierapolis
Manbij
SYRIA
Antioch
Aleppo
Halys
Euphrates
Euphrates

WHY WERE THE CRUSADES STARTED?

In the middle of the 11th century, the Selçuk Turks attacked and took over the Near East. They dominated the Arab power seat, which was the Abbasid Caliphate presiding over Baghdad. Then they moved both to the north and to the west and in the process they seized most of the land of the Byzantine Anatolia, which today is thought of as Asia Minor.

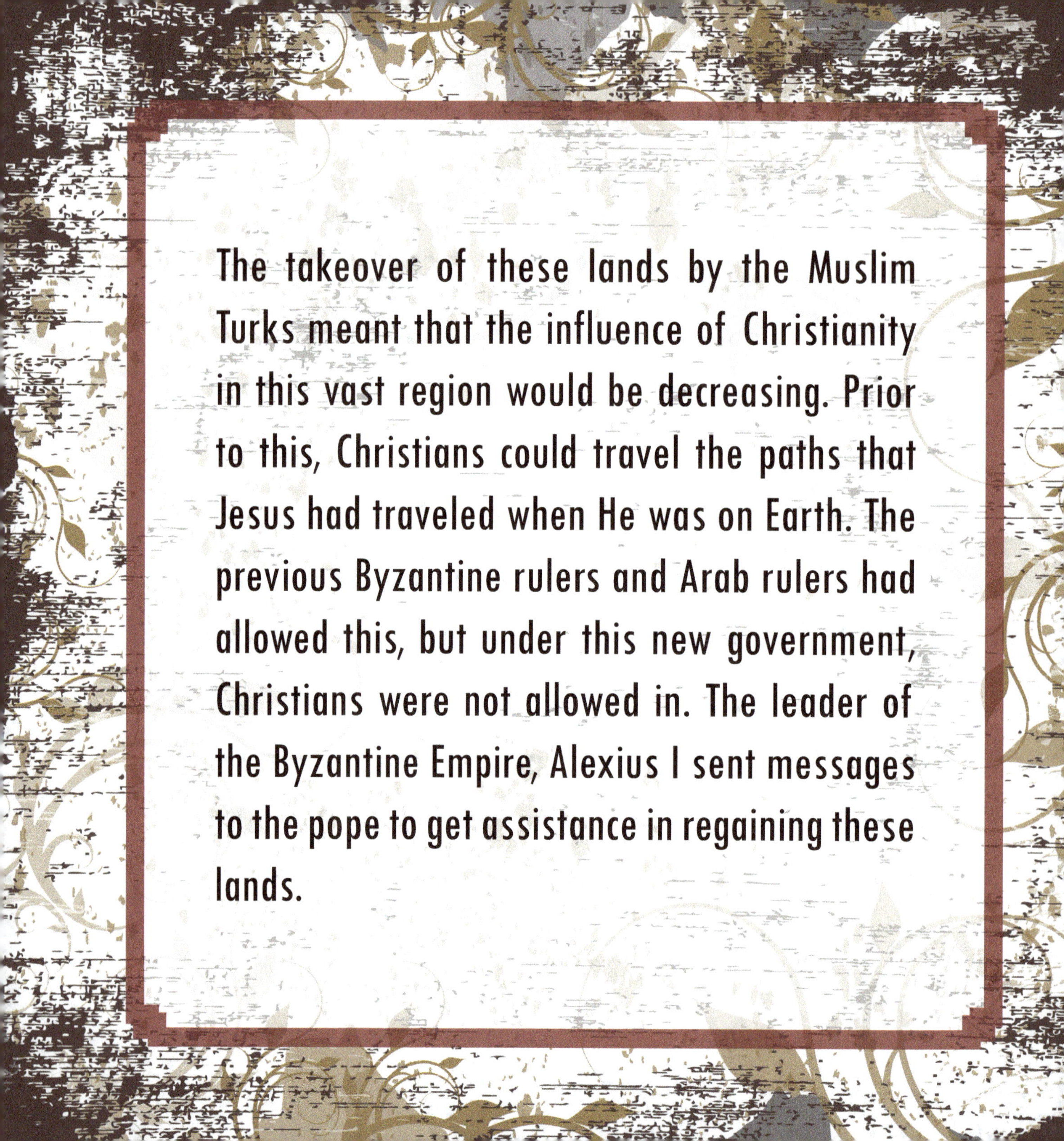

The takeover of these lands by the Muslim Turks meant that the influence of Christianity in this vast region would be decreasing. Prior to this, Christians could travel the paths that Jesus had traveled when He was on Earth. The previous Byzantine rulers and Arab rulers had allowed this, but under this new government, Christians were not allowed in. The leader of the Byzantine Empire, Alexius I sent messages to the pope to get assistance in regaining these lands.

Alexius 1

Pope Urban II speech

POPE URBAN II GIVES A SPEECH

Pope Urban II decided to give a speech to motivate the people to act in response to the Muslim takeover of the Holy Land. He delivered his rousing speech to the people in Clermont, a city in central France.

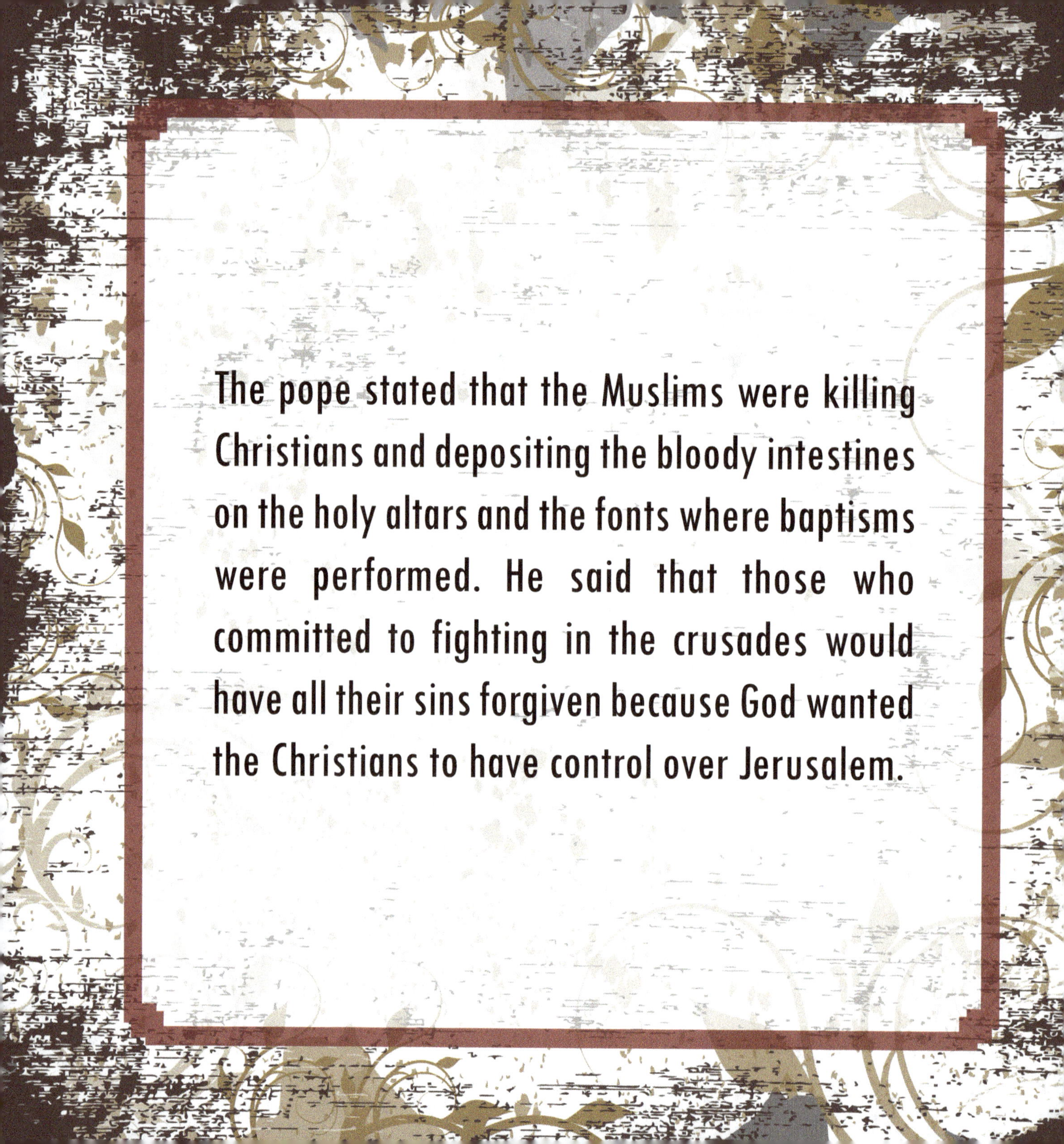

The pope stated that the Muslims were killing Christians and depositing the bloody intestines on the holy altars and the fonts where baptisms were performed. He said that those who committed to fighting in the crusades would have all their sins forgiven because God wanted the Christians to have control over Jerusalem.

Pope Urban II

Old Jerusalem Church

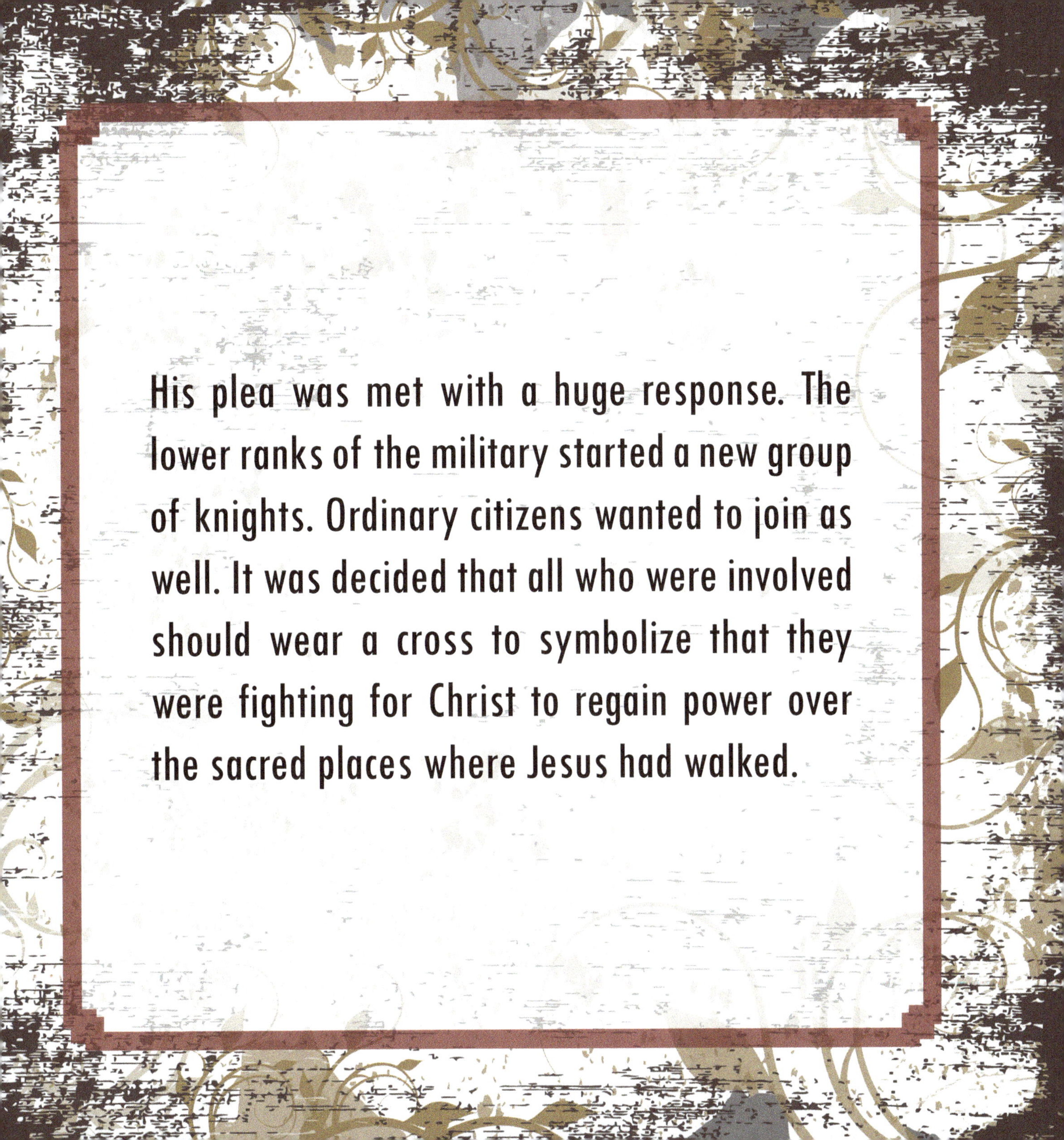

His plea was met with a huge response. The lower ranks of the military started a new group of knights. Ordinary citizens wanted to join as well. It was decided that all who were involved should wear a cross to symbolize that they were fighting for Christ to regain power over the sacred places where Jesus had walked.

THE FIRST CRUSADE (1096 AD to 1099 AD)

The royal families and the families of nobles gathered together the necessary funds for the Crusades and four armies were created from the different regions of Europe. In every case, a motley group of women, young children, and elderly people joined priests and peasants to travel with the knights on this holy quest.

1st Crusade

Pope Urban II Preaching the First Crusade

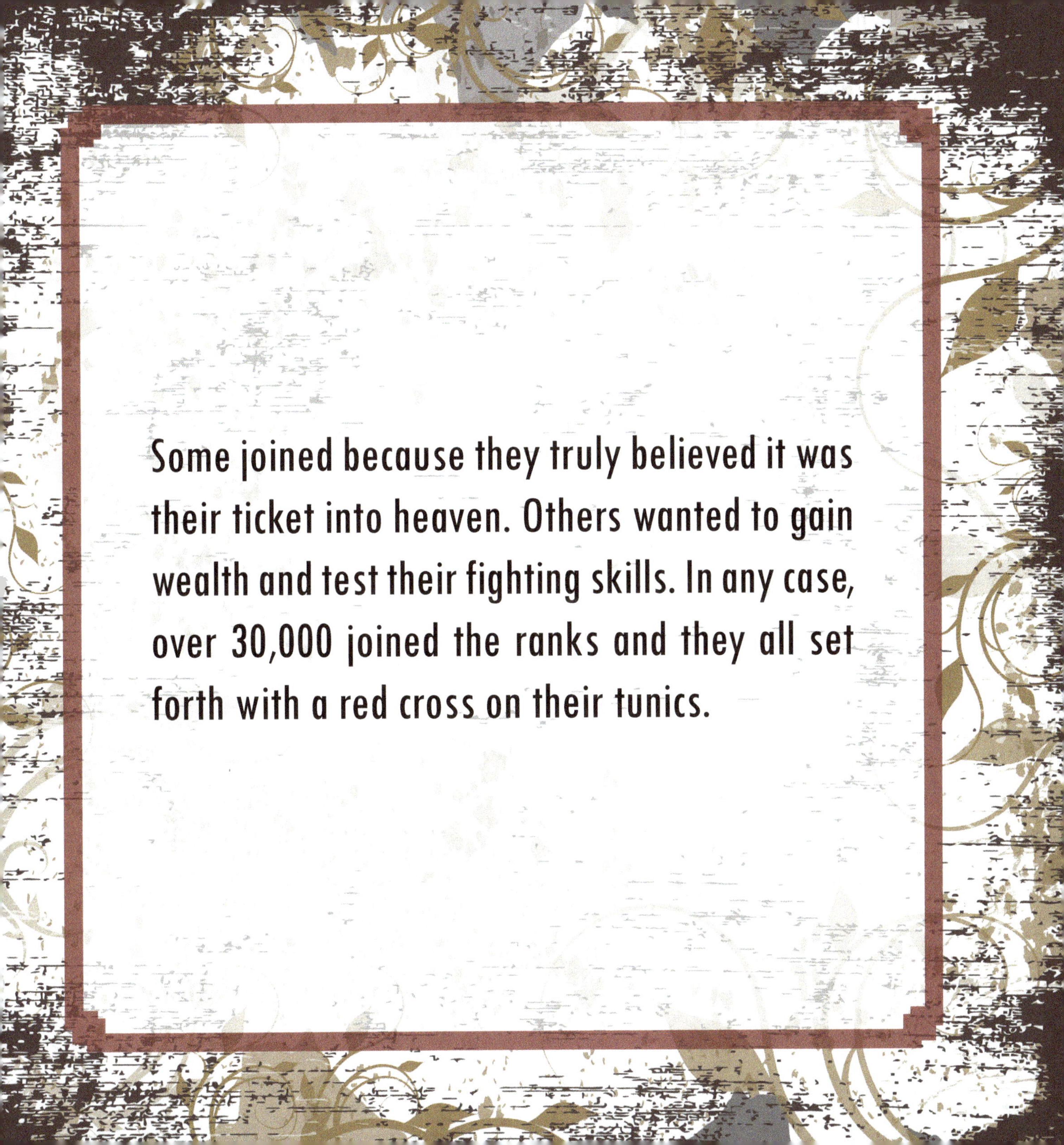

Some joined because they truly believed it was their ticket into heaven. Others wanted to gain wealth and test their fighting skills. In any case, over 30,000 joined the ranks and they all set forth with a red cross on their tunics.

These were the leaders of the different armies:

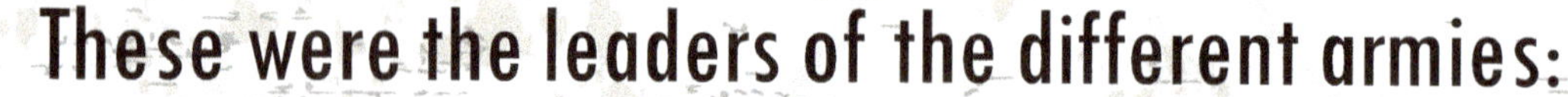

➦ Army 1: Raymond of Saint-Gilles, a powerful noble from Southern France

➦ Army 2: Godfrey of Bouillon, with his two brothers, Baldwin and Eustace

➦ Army 3: Hugh of Vermandois, the brother of the king of France

➦ Army 4: Bohemond of Taranto, along with Tancred, who was his nephew and who would eventually lead the capture of Jerusalem

Raymond de Saint Gilles

Crusade Leaders

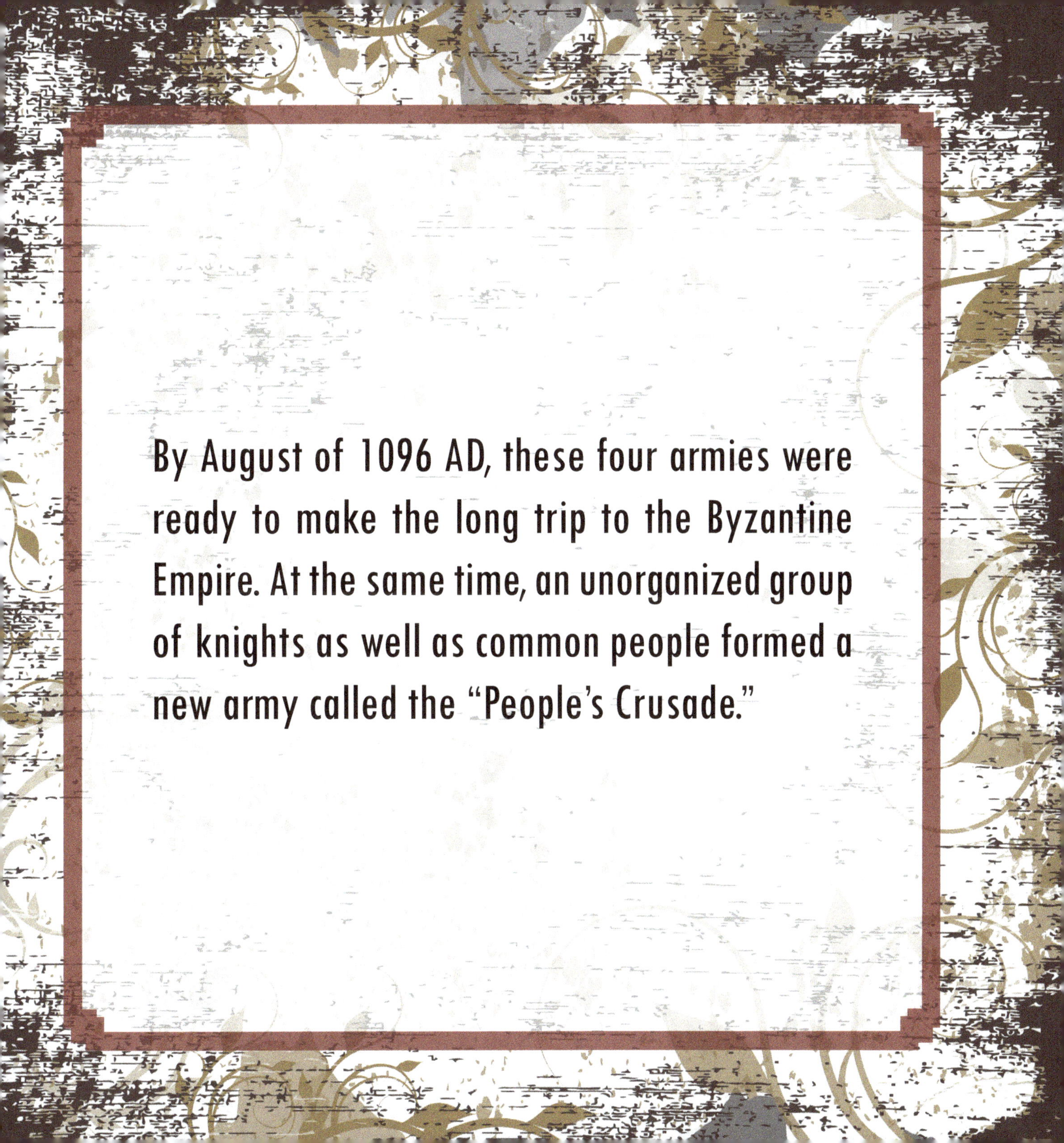

By August of 1096 AD, these four armies were ready to make the long trip to the Byzantine Empire. At the same time, an unorganized group of knights as well as common people formed a new army called the "People's Crusade."

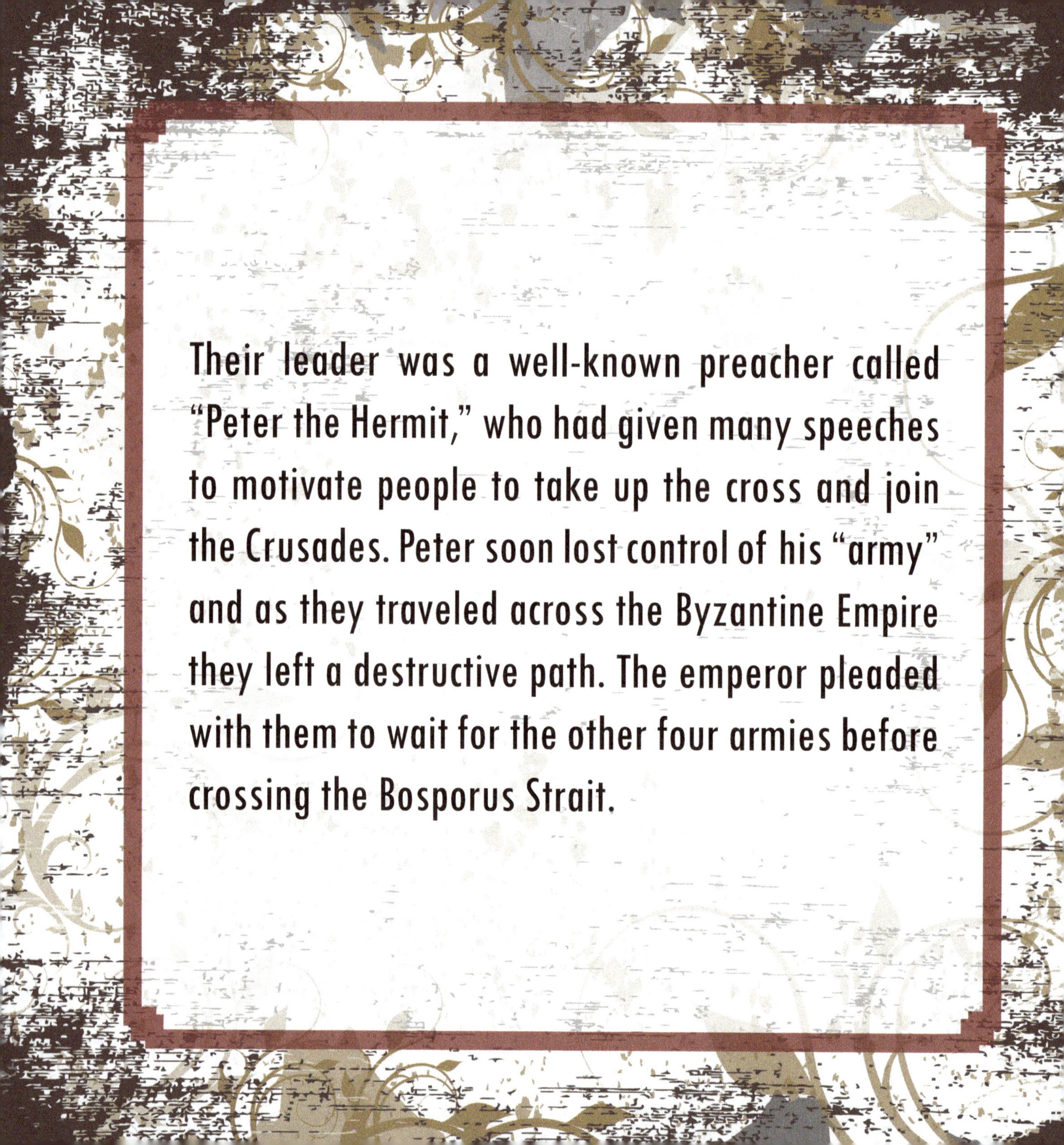

Their leader was a well-known preacher called "Peter the Hermit," who had given many speeches to motivate people to take up the cross and join the Crusades. Peter soon lost control of his "army" and as they traveled across the Byzantine Empire they left a destructive path. The emperor pleaded with them to wait for the other four armies before crossing the Bosporus Strait.

Army of Peter the Hermit

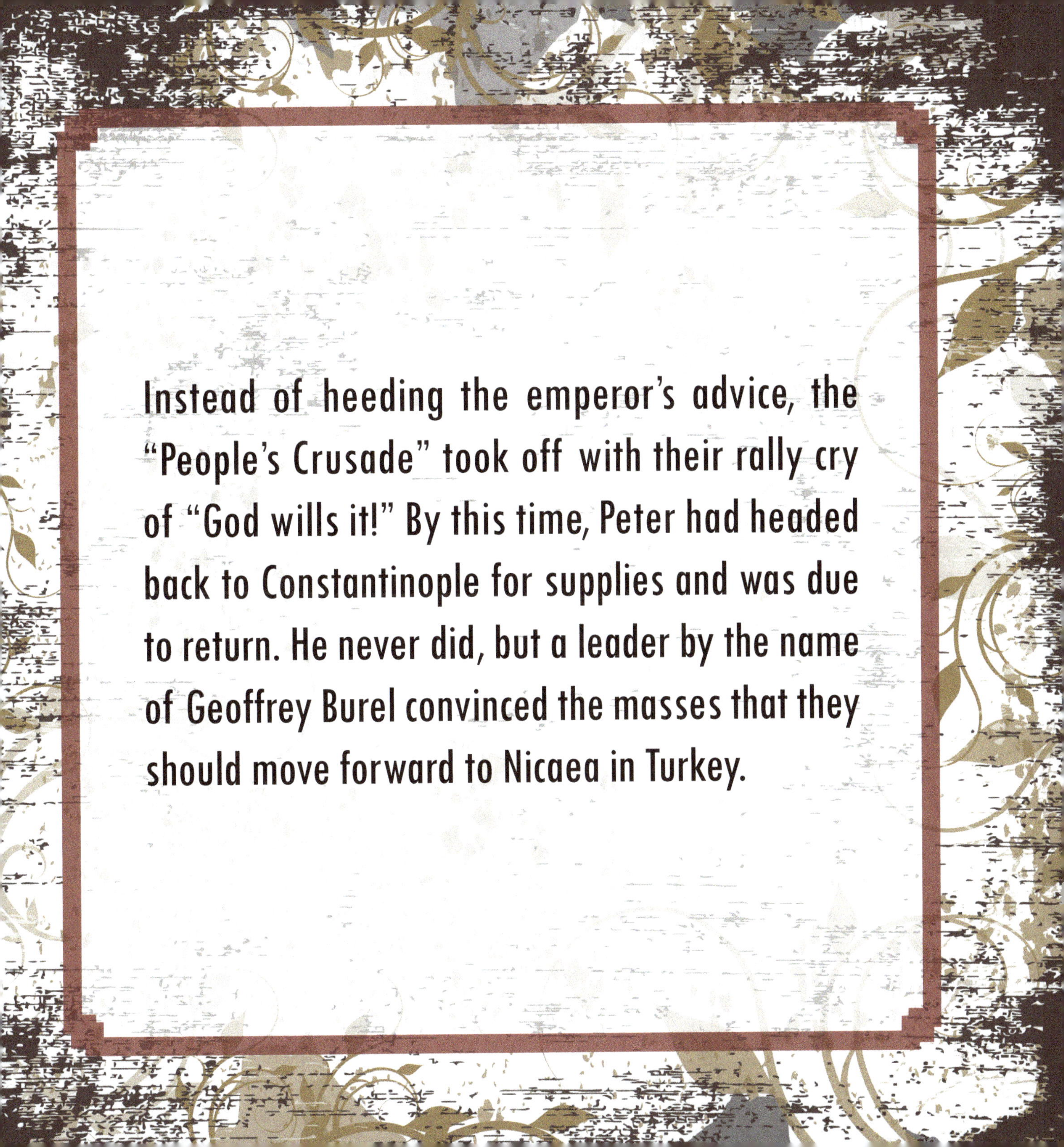

Instead of heeding the emperor's advice, the "People's Crusade" took off with their rally cry of "God wills it!" By this time, Peter had headed back to Constantinople for supplies and was due to return. He never did, but a leader by the name of Geoffrey Burel convinced the masses that they should move forward to Nicaea in Turkey.

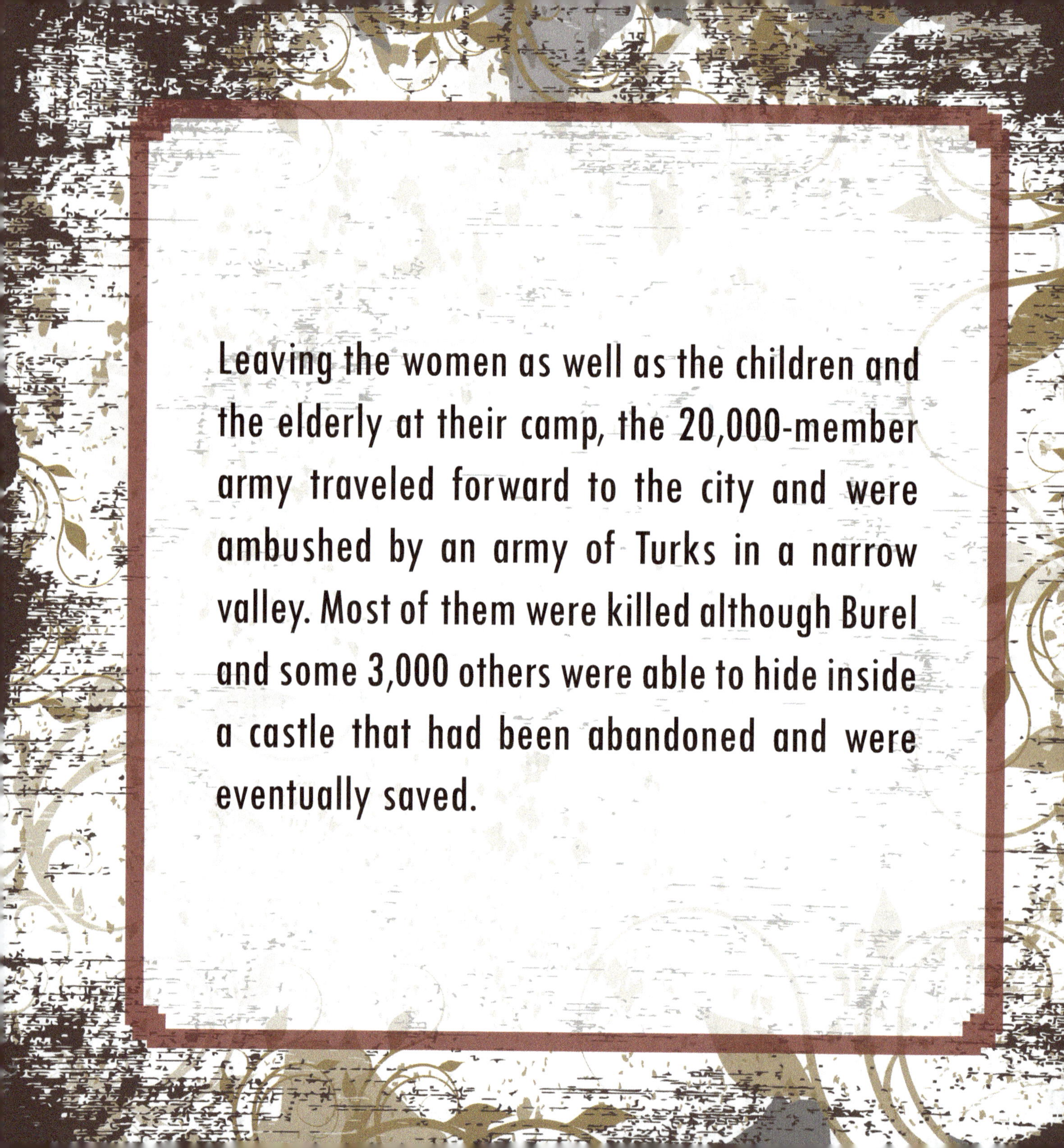

Leaving the women as well as the children and the elderly at their camp, the 20,000-member army traveled forward to the city and were ambushed by an army of Turks in a narrow valley. Most of them were killed although Burel and some 3,000 others were able to hide inside a castle that had been abandoned and were eventually saved.

Battle in front of Antioch

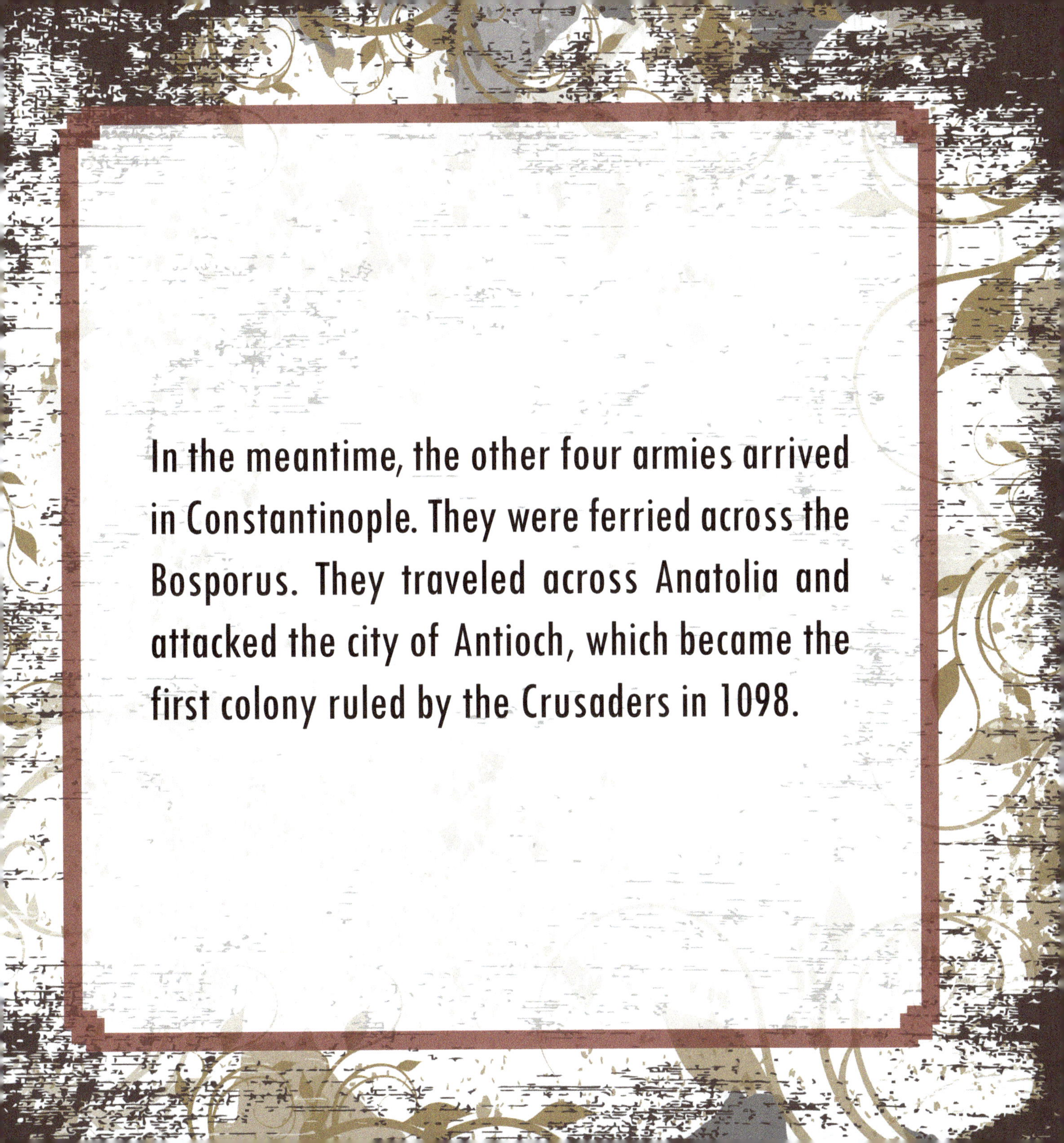

In the meantime, the other four armies arrived in Constantinople. They were ferried across the Bosporus. They traveled across Anatolia and attacked the city of Antioch, which became the first colony ruled by the Crusaders in 1098.

THE SIEGE OF JERUSALEM

After a two-week-long siege of the city of Jerusalem, in July of 1099 AD, Tancred led the crusaders through the northern wall of the city located near Herod's Gate. The rulers gave up without fighting and the city had been taken from Muslim control.

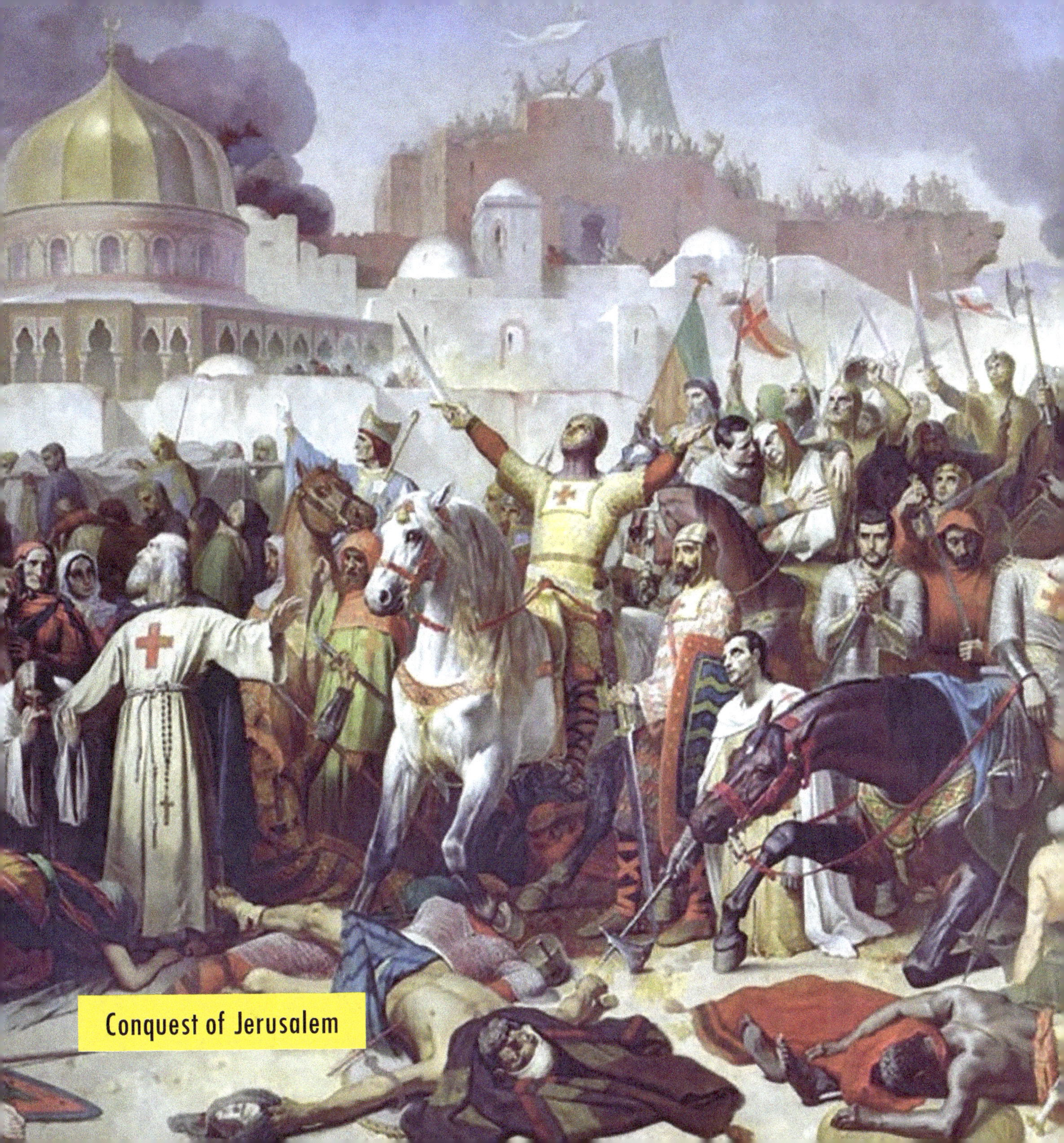

Conquest of Jerusalem

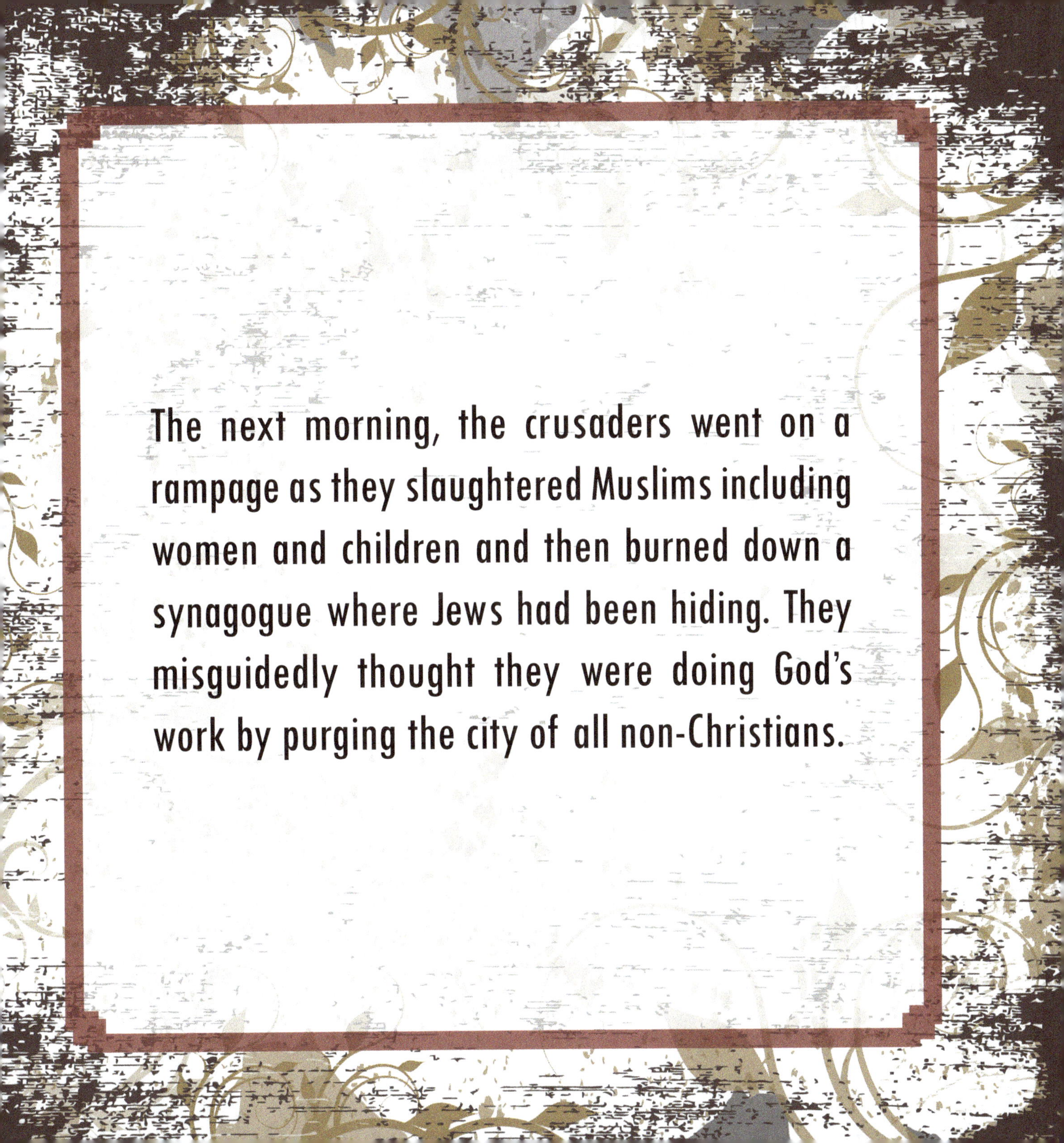

The next morning, the crusaders went on a rampage as they slaughtered Muslims including women and children and then burned down a synagogue where Jews had been hiding. They misguidedly thought they were doing God's work by purging the city of all non-Christians.

THE LATIN KINGDOM OF JERUSALEM

The Crusaders selected Godfrey of Bouillon to lead them, but he died a year later in 1100 AD and his brother Baldwin took over the now-called Latin Kingdom of Jerusalem. By the middle of the 12th century, this kingdom was ruling the land we now know as Israel as well as western Jordan and the southern region of Lebanon. However, the Crusaders didn't rule the city for long. They only held it for about 90 years. Of the many crusades, this first one was the most successful.

2nd Crusade

THE SECOND CRUSADE (1147 AD to 1149 AD)

The Turks invaded and conquered the city of Edessa in 1146 AD. The entire population of the city was either slaughtered or enslaved. A second Crusade was sent to conquer the city, but it was not victorious.

THE THIRD CRUSADE (1187 AD to 1192 AD)

The Sultan of Egypt, who was called Saladin, took Jerusalem away from Christian rule in 1187 AD. A third Crusade was sent with leaders from Germany, France, and England. Richard the Lionheart from England continued to fight Saladin for a number of years, but was unable to take Jerusalem back. He was able to negotiate the right for Christians to walk where Jesus had walked.

Saladin after battle of Hattin in 1187

Teutonic Knights

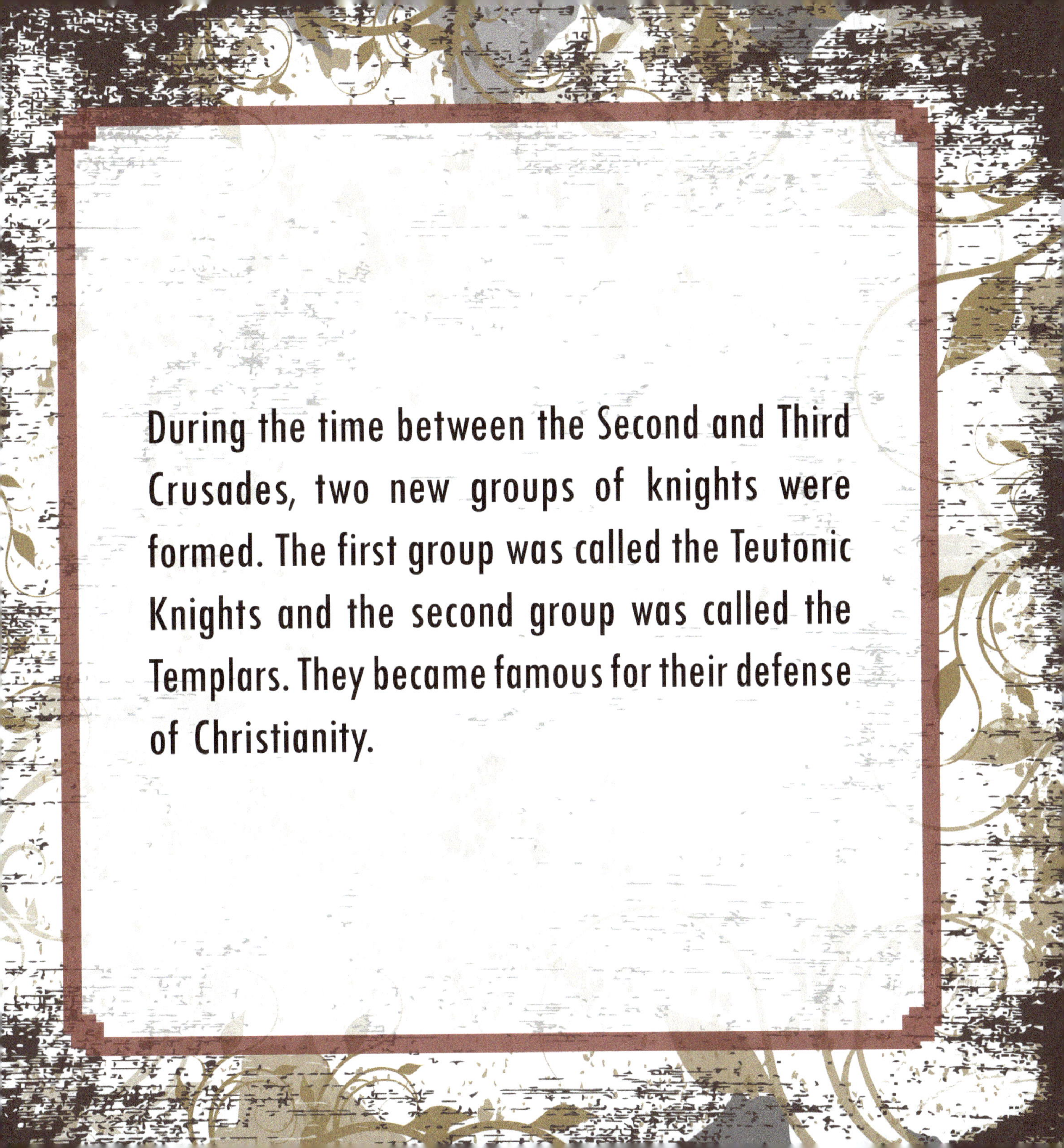

During the time between the Second and Third Crusades, two new groups of knights were formed. The first group was called the Teutonic Knights and the second group was called the Templars. They became famous for their defense of Christianity.

THE FOURTH CRUSADE (1202 AD to 1204 AD)

Pope Innocent III launched the next crusade but instead of gaining back the Holy Land, the participants ransacked the city of Constantinople.

4th Crusade

Childrens Crusade

CHILDREN'S CRUSADE (1212 AD)

The Children's Crusade came about when Stephen of Cloyes, a child in France, claimed to have received a message from God to march on to Jerusalem and reclaim it for Christianity. Meanwhile in Germany, another boy named Nicholas had made a similar claim.

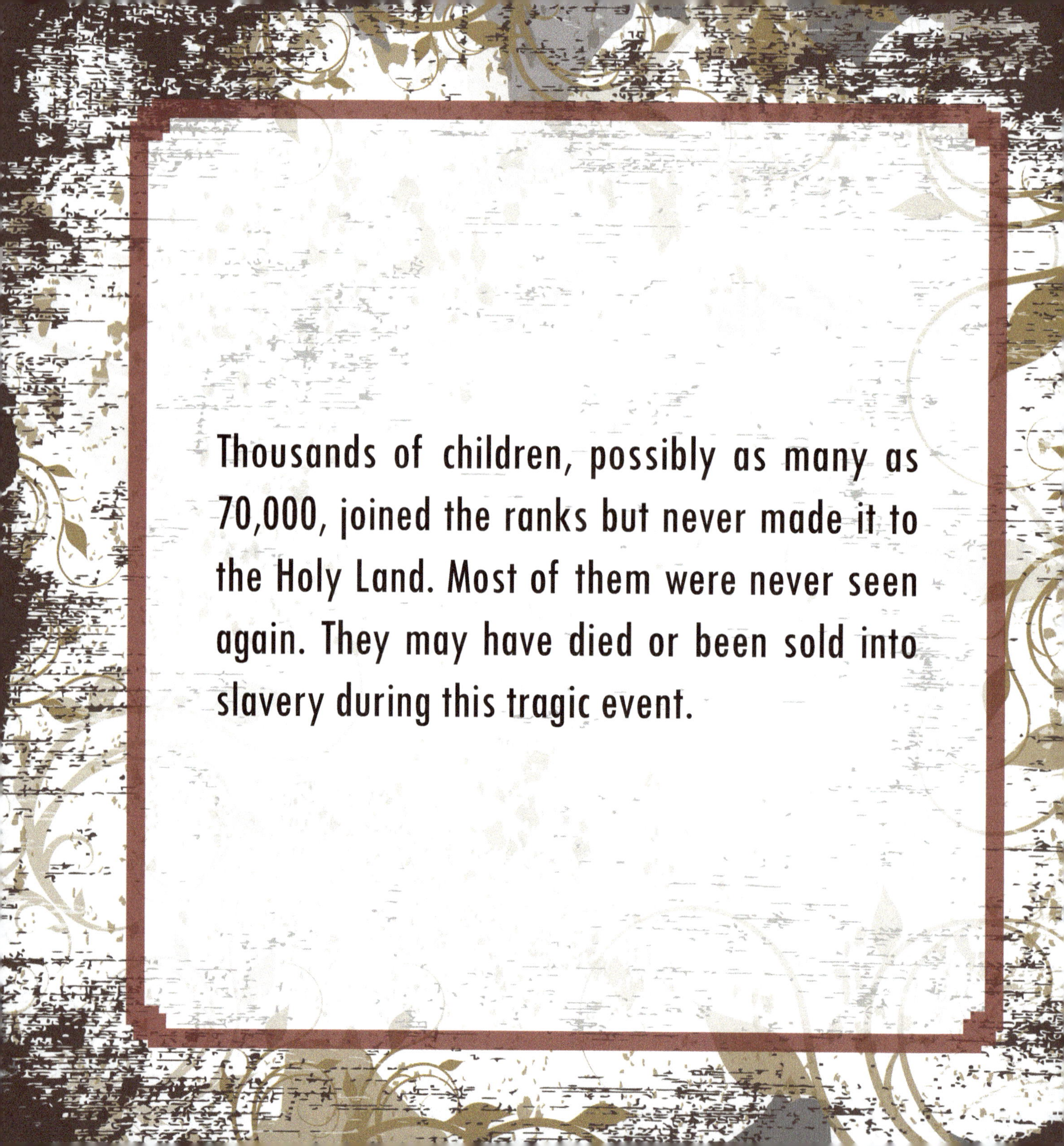

Thousands of children, possibly as many as 70,000, joined the ranks but never made it to the Holy Land. Most of them were never seen again. They may have died or been sold into slavery during this tragic event.

Holy Land

CRUSADES FIVE THROUGH NINE
(1217 AD to 1272 AD)

There were five more crusades after the Children's Crusade, but none of them were able to win back the Holy Land.

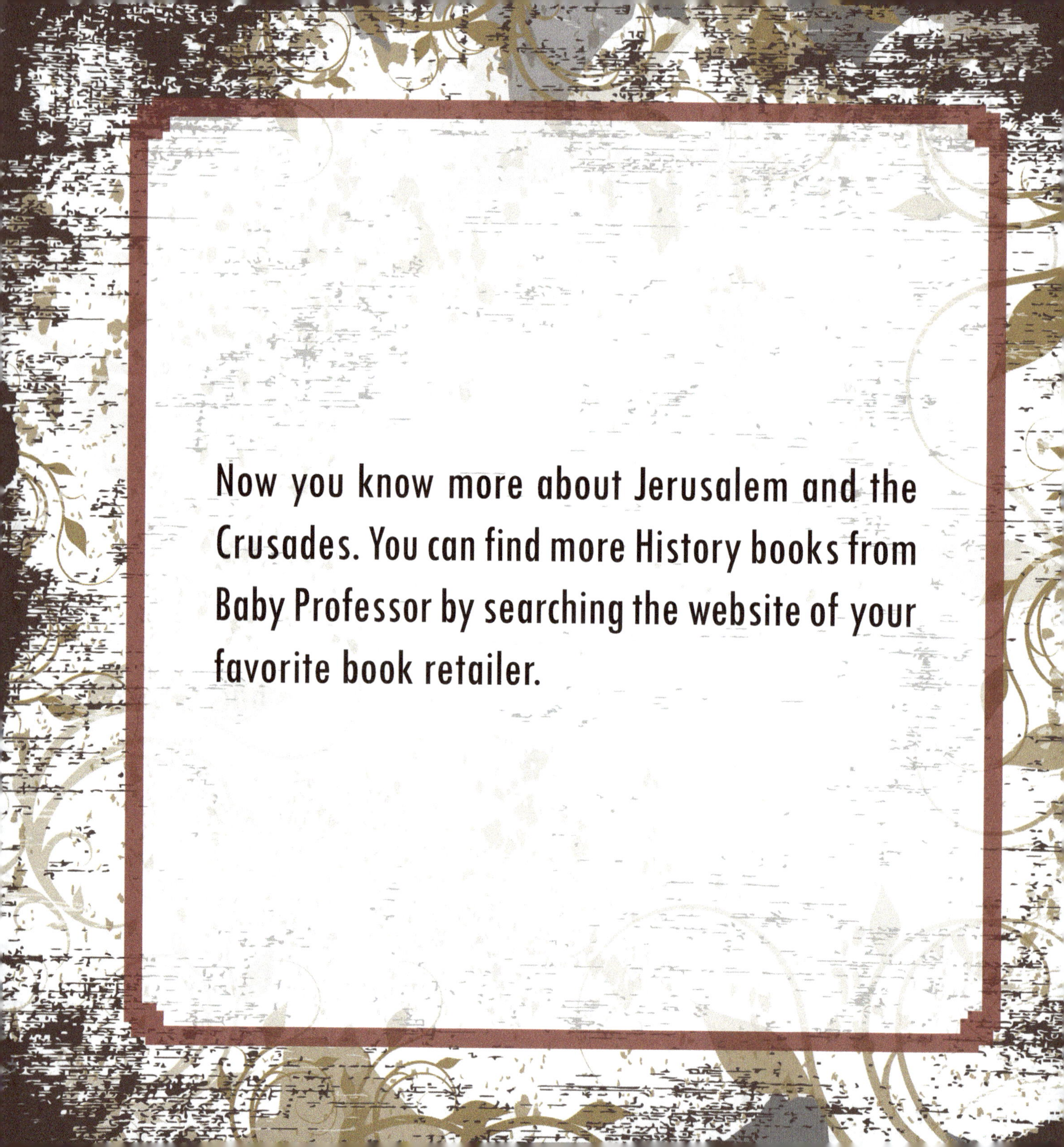

Now you know more about Jerusalem and the Crusades. You can find more History books from Baby Professor by searching the website of your favorite book retailer.

Old Jerusalem

Visit
BABY PROFESSOR
EDUCATION KIDS
www.BabyProfessorBooks.com
to download Free Baby Professor eBooks
and view our catalog of new and exciting
Children's Books